STADIUM DESIGN

daab

Introduction 4

In ancient Greece, the term stadium was defined as a footrace over a distance of 192 m. This distance measurement was then later used as a description for the competition facility. Nowadays a stadium is considered a total competitive sporting complex with field, oval-shaped running track, shotput, javelin and broad jump facilities as well as viewer seats and press boxes. The shape of a stadium is determined by its purpose. In this case, one can differentiate between two-tier baseball stadia, riding and horseracing stadia as well as existing primary and secondary-tier racecar stadia. The pure football stadia, on the other hand, are composed of four straight seating terraces, which are configured around a rectangular playing field. They are generally open, but may have opening roofs or may even be completely covered. Sometimes membranes are also used for the roof construction; these are usually polyester-coated fabrics which are, consequently, very durable and tear-resistant. In the case of multi-purpose stadia, the seating stands are arranged in an oval manner around the lawn in order to equip the stadium with a running track and landing area. Nowadays, stadia are not simply sporting sites, but also act as tourist attractions, distinguishing features and gathering place for clubs. This tendency has led to increased value being placed upon architecture in stadium design. The concept of a stadium signifies a large challenge, since various functions must be integrated into a single complex. Within a very short period of time, a stadium must receive a large number of visitors. It must offer safety from the wind and weather and do so with large construction areas which are, however, equipped with very few materials. Especially in the case of football stadia, regulations of the international football association, FIFA highly standardize the seating terrace space. For this reason, stadia look more and more alike in indoors. Differences are reduced primarily to the exterior skin, the color of the seats and the roof construction. Since the construction of a stadium is very expensive, often stadia are conceived for a second use as concert arena. Additional uses for covered stadia may include stores, offices, hotels and restaurants. In the following, various solutions of modern stadia design are presented. In so doing, examples of various use types and sizes will be addressed.

Im antiken Griechenland definierte man mit dem Begriff Stadion zunächst den über eine Distanz von 192 m ausgetragenen Wettlauf. Dieses Längenmaß wurde dann später als Bezeichnung für die Wettkampfanlage übernommen. Heutzutage versteht man unter Stadion die Gesamtanlage einer Wettkampfbahn für sportliche Zwecke mit Rasenplatz, ovaler Laufbahn, Wurf- und Sprunganlagen sowie Zuschauer- und Pressetribünen. Die Form eines Stadions wird jeweils von seinem Zweck bestimmt. So kann man zwischen zweischenkligen Baseballstadien, Reit- und Pferderennstadien sowie aus Haupt- und Nebentribünen bestehenden Autorennstadien unterscheiden. Die reinen Fußballstadien hingegen bestehen aus vier geraden Tribünen, die um ein rechteckiges Spielfeld angeordnet sind. Sie sind in der Regel offen, können jedoch auch öffnende Dächer besitzen oder sogar vollständig überdacht sein. Oft werden für die Dachkonstruktionen auch Membranen verwendet; das sind meist mit Polyester beschichtete Gewebe, die dadurch sehr beständig und reißfest werden. Bei Mehrzweckstadien werden die Tribünen oval um die Rasenfläche angeordnet, um das Stadion mit Laufbahn und Sprunggrube auszustatten. Stadien sind heutzutage nicht einfach nur Sportstätten, sondern agieren auch als Touristenattraktion, Erkennungszeichen und Ort des Zusammentreffens für die Klubs. Diese Tendenz hat zu einer Aufwertung der Architektur im Stadionbau geführt. Die Konzeption eines Stadions bedeutet eine große Herausforderung, da unterschiedlichste Funktionsbereiche in einen Komplex integriert werden müssen. Innerhalb kürzester Zeit muß ein Stadion eine große Anzahl an Besuchern aufnehmen. Es muß Sicherheit bei Wind und Wetter bieten und das bei großen Konstruktionsflächen, die aber mit sehr wenig Material ausgestaltet werden. Speziell bei Fußballstadien führen die Normen des Weltfußballverbandes FIFA zu einer starken Standardisierung des Tribünenraums. Dadurch gleichen sich die Stadien im Innenraum immer mehr an. Die Unterschiede reduzieren sich hauptsächlich auf die Außenhaut, die Farbgebung der Sitze und die Dachkonstruktion. Da der Bau eines Stadions mit enormen Kosten verbunden ist, werden die Stadien häufig auch für eine Zweitnutzung als Konzertarena konzipiert. Eine weitere Möglichkeit besteht in der Mantelnutzung mit Geschäften, Büros, Hotels und Restaurants. Im folgenden werden verschiede Lösungen des modernen Stadienbaus vorgestellt. Dabei werden Beispiele verschiedenster Nutzungsarten und −größen berücksichtigt.

Dans l'Antiquité grecque, le terme de Stadion définissait la longueur de la piste pour la compétition, à savoir 192 m. Cette unité de longueur a été utilisée plus tard pour définir le lieu de la compétition. Aujourd'hui, le stade est l'endroit où toutes les compétitions sportives ont lieu, disposant d'une pelouse, d'une piste en forme d'ellipse, d'installations de lancer et de saut ainsi que de tribunes pour les spectateurs et le service de presse. La forme du stade découle naturellement de son utilisation. On distingue alors plusieurs types de stades: le stade de basket-ball, les hippodromes et les circuits de course de voitures avec les tribunes principales et annexes. Quant aux stades de football, ils possèdent quatre tribunes droites implantées autour d'un terrain de jeu carré. Ils sont en général à ciel ouvert ou doté d'un toit ouvrant ou encore complètement couverts. Les couvertures sont souvent remplacées par une membrane, faite en général de toile de polyester enduite, offrant ainsi une résistance à tout épreuve. Dans le cas de stades polyvalents, les tribunes sont implantées en ellipse autour du gazon pour installer les pistes de course et les fosses pour le saut. De nos jours, les stades ne sont plus uniquement des cités sportives, ce sont aussi des pôles touristiques, emblèmes et points de rencontre des clubs. Cette tendance amène à une revalorisation architecturale des stades dont la conception représente un énorme défi, vu la multiplicité des fonctions qui, aujourd'hui, doivent y être intégrées. En un temps record, les stades doivent pouvoir accueillir un grand nombre de visiteurs et aussi les protéger des intempéries. Ce qui n'est pas évident vu leur grande envergure et le peu de matériel employé. Quant aux stades de football, les normes définies par la FIFA, association mondiale du football, conduisent à une standardisation accrue des espaces réservés aux tribunes. Les stades se ressemblent donc de plus en plus, les seules différences étant surtout visibles au niveau de la structure extérieure, de la couleur des sièges et de la couverture. La construction des stades étant très coûteuse, ils sont souvent polyvalents et utilisés comme salle de concert, ou accueillent dans leur enceinte, commerces, bureaux, hôtels et restaurants. Au fil des pages de cet ouvrage, vous découvrirez une gamme variée de propositions de construction de stade offrant tout un éventail de modèles de tailles et d'utilisations diverses.

En la antigua Grecia el término estadio se aplicaba a una prueba deportiva que consistía en correr una distancia de 192 m. Esta medida de longitud pasó a definir por extensión el lugar donde se celebraban esas carreras. En nuestros días, los estadios albergan un conjunto de espacios: un campo de hierba, una pista de atletismo, varias pistas de lanzamiento y salto, gradas y tribunas para público y prensa. La forma de un estadio es determinada por su función principal; podemos distinguir entre estadios de béisbol de dos alas, hipódromos y recintos para competiciones hípicas, y circuitos para carreras de coches con tribunas principales y gradas accesorias. Los estadios consagrados únicamente al fútbol suelen tener cuatro zonas de gradas que flanquean un campo de juego de forma cuadrangular. Por lo general, estas zonas no están cubiertas, pero en ocasiones pueden estar protegidas por paneles extensibles o, incluso, estar totalmente techadas. Habitualmente para este tipo de cubiertas se utiliza un tejido recubierto de poliéster muy resistente. En el caso de los estadios concebidos para desempeñar distintas funciones, las gradas ciñen la superficie del césped y las pistas de atletismo y de salto. Sin lugar a dudas, los estadios actuales ya no son meros complejos deportivos, sino una atracción turística y un símbolo de sus clubes, además de un lugar de encuentro; una situación, esta, que ha llevado a una revalorización de su arquitectura. De hecho, el proyecto de este tipo de construcciones supone siempre un reto, ya que los diferentes ámbitos funcionales deben integrarse en un único complejo; además, un estadio tiene que ser capaz de acoger un número enorme de visitantes en un corto espacio de tiempo y protegerlos de las condiciones atmosféricas adversas. Las normas de la FIFA han hecho que los estadios de fútbol se caractericen por una marcada estandarización del espacio de tribunas; por esta razón, el espacio interior de estas construcciones se parece cada vez más y las diferencias se concentran en el aspecto exterior, en el color de los asientos y en la forma de las cubiertas. Debido a sus elevados costes de construcción, al proyectar un estadio se tienen en cuenta también futuros usos polivalentes, como la posibilidad de acoger conciertos o la de albergar, en su perímetro exterior, comercios, oficinas, hoteles y restaurantes. En las páginas que siguen se presentan modernos proyectos de estadios, pensados para responder a diversas necesidades y adaptarse a múltiples funciones y escalas.

Nell'antica Grecia il termine stadio definiva inizialmente una gara di corsa su una distanza di 192 m. Questa misura divenne successivamente la denominazione della struttura in cui si svolgeva la gara. Oggi lo stadio rappresenta un impianto per competizioni sportive con campo erboso, pista ovale da corsa, impianti per il salto e il lancio e tribune stampa e per gli spettatori. La forma di uno stadio è definita in base alle sua finalità. È possibile infatti distinguere tra stadi di baseball, stadi per l'equitazione e stadi per le corse automobilistiche con tribune principali e secondarie. Gli stadi da calcio, invece, comprendono quattro tribune dritte, collocate intorno a un campo da calcio rettangolare. Esse possiedono solitamente una struttura aperta, anche se possono avere tettoie apribili o addirittura essere completamente coperte. Spesso gli elementi di copertura sono composti da membrane, realizzate con reti rivestite di poliestere per essere più resistenti. In stadi multifunzionali, le tribune sono disposte in maniera ovale intorno al campo da calcio, per lasciare spazio alla pista d'atletica e alla buca del salto in lungo. Al giorno d'oggi, gli stadi non sono soltanto impianti sportivi ma fungono anche da attrazione turistica, segno di riconoscimento e luogo d'incontro per i club. Questa tendenza ha portato a una rivalutazione dell'architettura degli stadi. La fase di progettazione rappresenta infatti una grande sfida poiché i settori più diversi devono essere integrati in un complesso unitario. Uno stadio deve accogliere in pochissimo tempo un numero consistente di visitatori e deve offrire sicurezza anche in caso di vento e pioggia, su superfici dalle grandi dimensioni realizzate con una quantità limitata di materiali. Per quanto riguarda gli stadi da calcio, le normative della Federazione Internazionale FIFA hanno portato a un'elevata standardizzazione della struttura delle tribune, per cui gli spazi interni si somigliano in maniera sempre più spiccata. Le differenze si riducono principalmente all'involucro esterno, ai colori dei sedili e alla copertura. Siccome la costruzione di uno stadio comporta enormi costi, spesso si realizza una struttura per un impiego differenziato, per esempio che funga anche da arena per concerti. Un'altra possibilità prevede l'utilizzo degli spazi verso l'esterno con negozi, uffici, hotel e ristoranti. Di seguito vi presentiamo diverse soluzioni per la realizzazione di moderni stadi, con modalità d'impiego eterogenee e dimensioni estremamente differenziate.

ARCHITEKTEN ARAT-SIEGEL & PARTNER, SCHLAICH BERGERMANN & PARTNER, WEIDLEPLAN CONSULTING | STUTTGART

GOTTLIEB-DAIMLER STADIUM
www.gottlieb-daimler-stadion.de
Stuttgart, Germany | 2005

ARCHITEKTEN SCHRÖDER SCHULTE-LADBECK STROTHMANN | DORTMUND
WESTFALEN STADIUM
www.bvb.de
Dortmund, Germany | 2004

ATELIER D'ARCHITECTURE CHAIX & MOREL ET ASSOCIÉS | PARIS
LICORNE AMIENS STADIUM
www.amiensfoot.com
Amiens, France | 1999

ATELIER HITOSHI ABE | **MIYAGI**

MIYAGI WORLD CUP STADIUM
www.pref.miyagi.jp
Miyagi, Japan | 2001

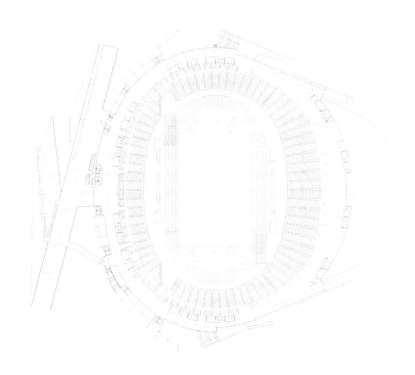

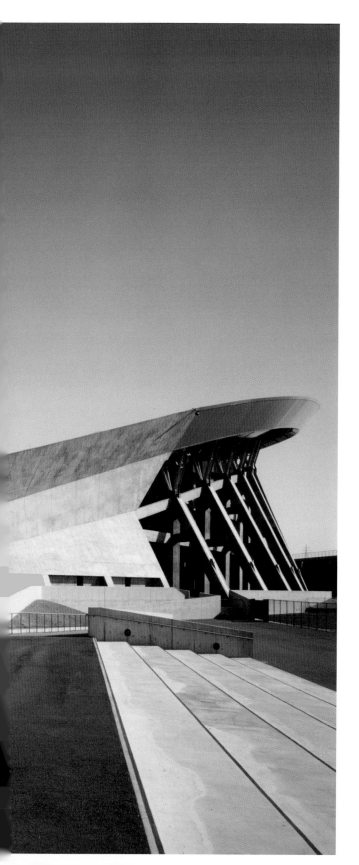

AXS SATOW | **TOKYO**
SHIZUOKA STADIUM
www.s-pulse.co.jp
Shizuoka, Japan | 2001

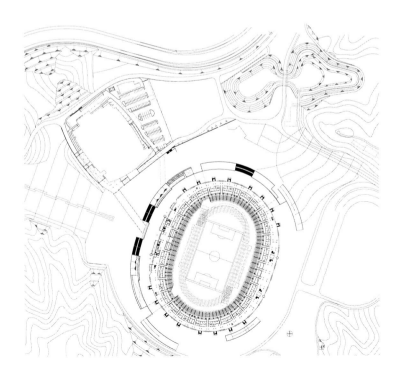

BEYOND SPACE GROUP/CHOON-SOO RYU | SEOUL
SEOUL WORLD CUP MAIN STADIUM
www.seoulworldcupst.or.kr
Seoul, South Korea | 2002

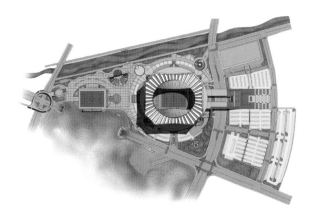

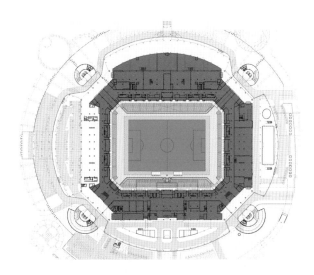

DOMINIQUE PERRAULT | PARIS
BERLIN OLYMPIC VELODROME
www.velodrom.de
Berlin, Germany | 1999

EDUARDO SOUTO DE MOURA | PORTO

BRAGA STADIUM
www.scbraga.com
Braga, Portugal | 2003

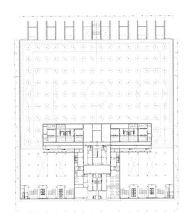

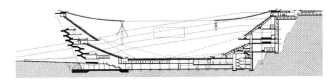

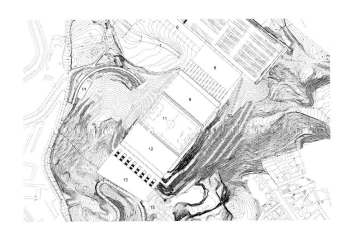

HENTRICH-PETSCHNIGG & PARTNER | DÜSSELDORF
FRANKEN STADIUM
www.franken-stadion.de
Nuremberg, Germany | 2005

HENTRICH-PETSCHNIGG & PARTNER | DÜSSELDORF

VELTINS ARENA
www.veltins-arena.de
Gelsenkirchen, Germany | 2001

THE UNION OF EUROPEAN FOOTBALL ASSOCIATIONS
CERTIFIES THAT

AUFSCHALKE

IS CLASSIFIED 5 STARS IN THE UEFA LIST OF STADIA

WE CARE ABOUT FOOTBALL

UEFA PRESIDENT

MAY 2004

LENNART JOHANSSON

weitere
Sitzplätze!

HERZOG & DE MEURON | BASEL

ALLIANZ ARENA
www.allianz-arena.de
Munich, Germany | 2005

HOK SPORT & VENUE & EVENT | KANSAS CITY
AMERICAN BALL PARK
www.reds.com
Cincinnati, Ohio, USA | 2003

HOK SPORT & VENUE & EVENT | KANSAS CITY
GILLETTE STADIUM
www.gillettestadium.com
Foxborough, Massachusetts, USA | 2002

IDEA IMAGE INSTITUTE OF ARCHITECTS / CHUL HEE KANG | SEOUL
DAEGU WORLD CUP STADIUM
www.daegufc.co.kr
Daegu, South Korea | 2003

KISHO KUROKAWA ARCHITECT & ASSOCIATES | TOKYO

OITA WORLD CUP STADIUM
www.bigeye.jp
Oita, Japan | 2001

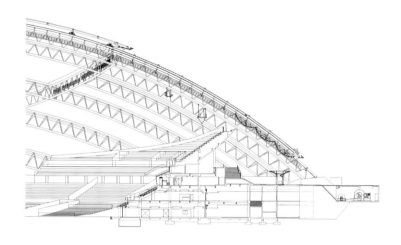

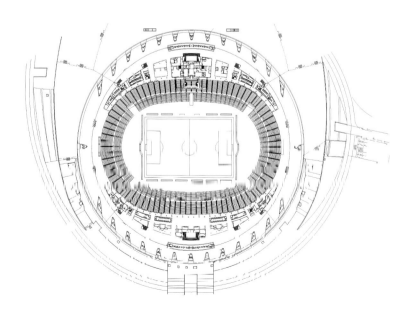

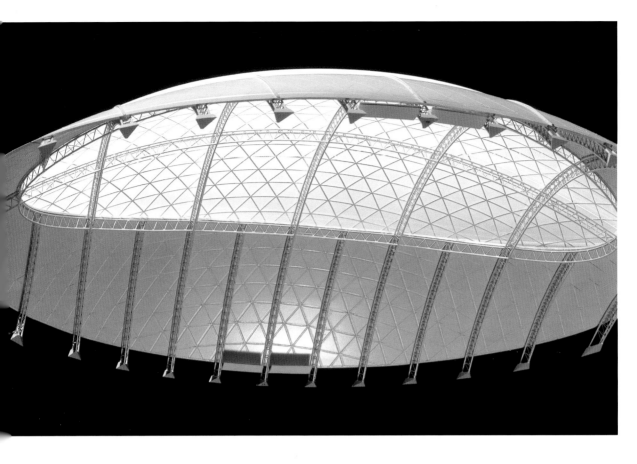

KISHO KUROKAWA ARCHITECT & ASSOCIATES | TOKYO

TOYOTA CITY STADIUM
www.toyota-stadium.co.jp
Toyota, Japan | 2001

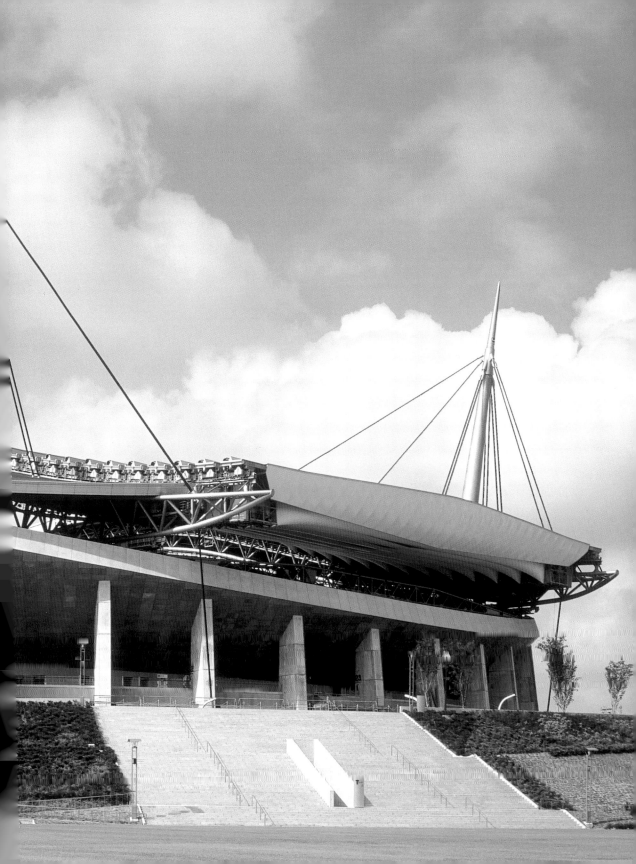

MANUEL SALGADO | **LISBON**

DRAGÃO STADIUM

www.fcporto.pt

Porto, Portugal | 2003

MOS ARCHITEKTEN | HAMBURG

AOL ARENA
www.hsv-aolarena.de
Hamburg, Germany | 2000

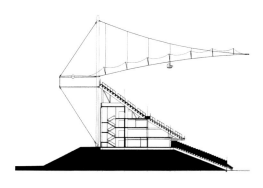

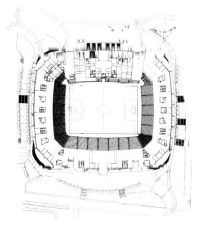

NIKKEN SEKKEI | TOKYO
BIG SWAN NIIGATA STADIUM
www.pref.niigata.jp
Niigata, Japan | 2002

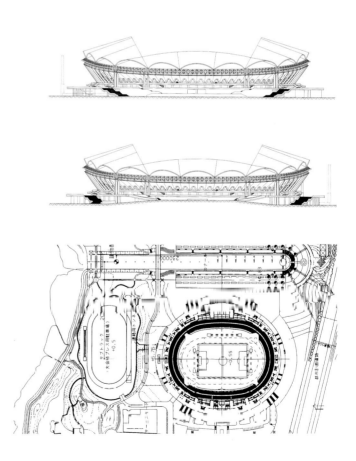

233

NOMAD ARQUITECTOS/EDUARDO ARROYO | MADRID

LOSEBARRE FOOTBALL STADIUM

www.barakaldocf.com
Barakaldo | 2003

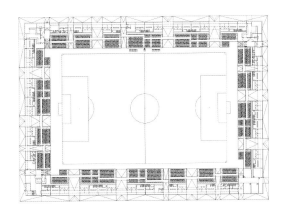

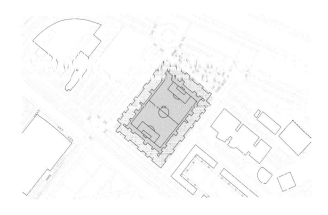

SANTIAGO CALATRAVA | ZURICH
ATHEN OLYMPIC STADIUM
www.athens2004.com
Athens, Greece | 2004

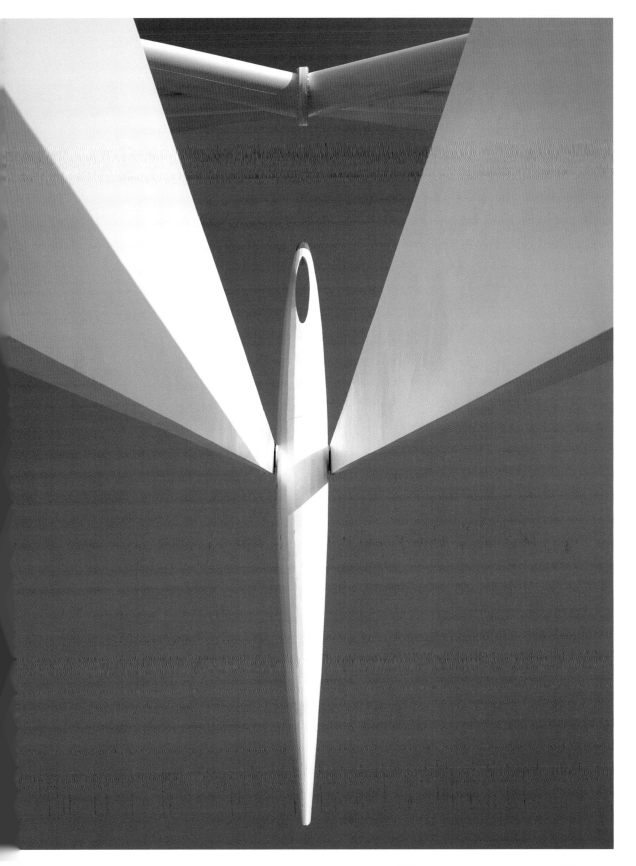

SANTIAGO CALATRAVA | ZURICH
ATHEN OLYMPIC VELODROME
www.athens2004.com
Athens, Greece | 2004

SCHULITZ & PARTNER ARCHITEKTEN | BRAUNSCHWEIG
AWD ARENA
www.awd-arena.de
Hannover, Germany | 2005

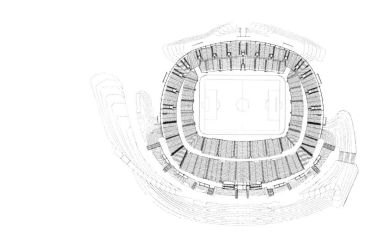

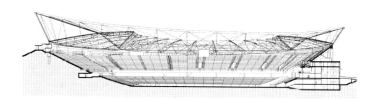

SPACE GROUP ARCHITECTS | SEOUL
BUSAN ASIAD MAIN STADIUM
www.busanworldcup.net
Busan Gwangyeoksi, South Korea | 2001

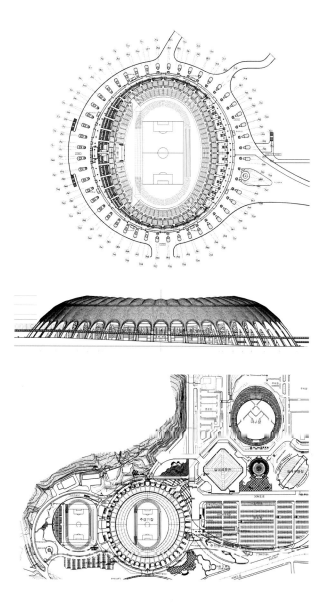

TOMÁS TAVEIRA | LISBOA

AVEIRO STADIUM

www.beiramar.pt

Aveiro, Portugal | 2003

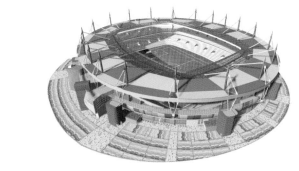

PORTA
DOOR
3

TOMÁS TAVEIRA | LISBON
JOSÉ ALVALADE XXI STADIUM
www.sporting.pt
Lisbon, Portugal | 2000

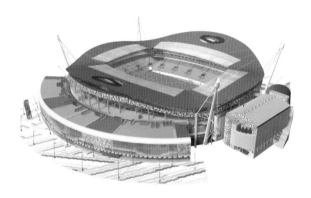

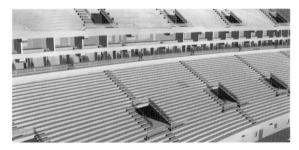

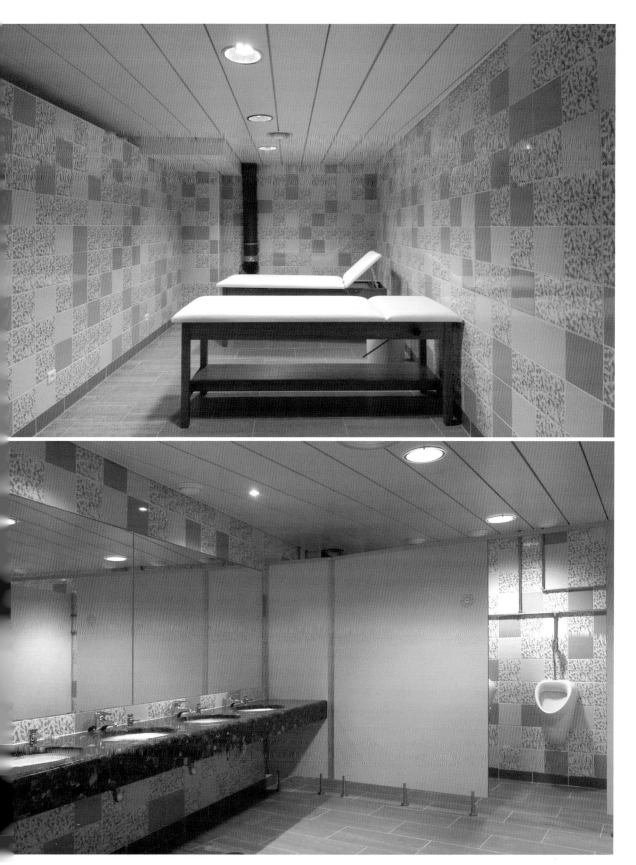

VON GERKAN, MARG & PARTNER | HAMBURG

BERLIN OLYMPIA STADIUM
www.olympiastadion-berlin.de
Berlin, Germany | 2004

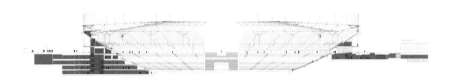

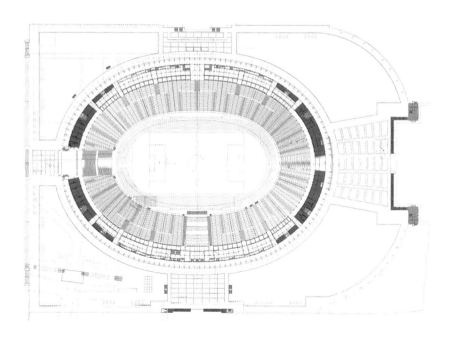

VON GERKAN, MARG & PARTNER | HAMBURG
COMMERZBANK ARENA
www.commerzbank-arena.de
Frankfurt, Germany | 2004

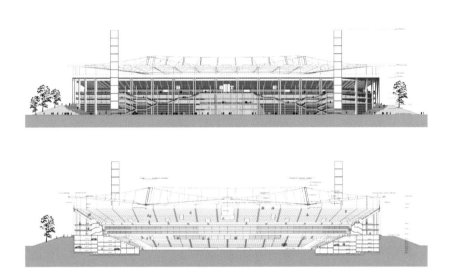

VON GERKAN, MARG & PARTNER | HAMBURG
RHEIN-ENERGY STADIUM
www.ctadion-koeln.de
Cologne, Germany | 2004

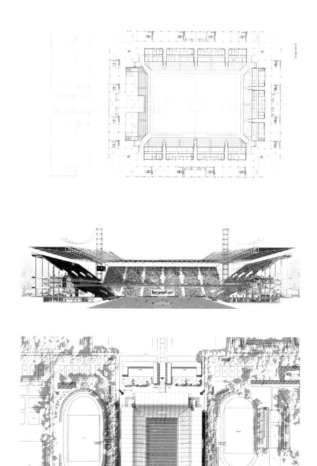

Tribüne Nord

WIRTH A WIRTH ARQUITEKTEN | LEIPZIG
ZENTRAL STADIUM
www.sportforum-leipzig.de
Leipzig, Germany | 2003

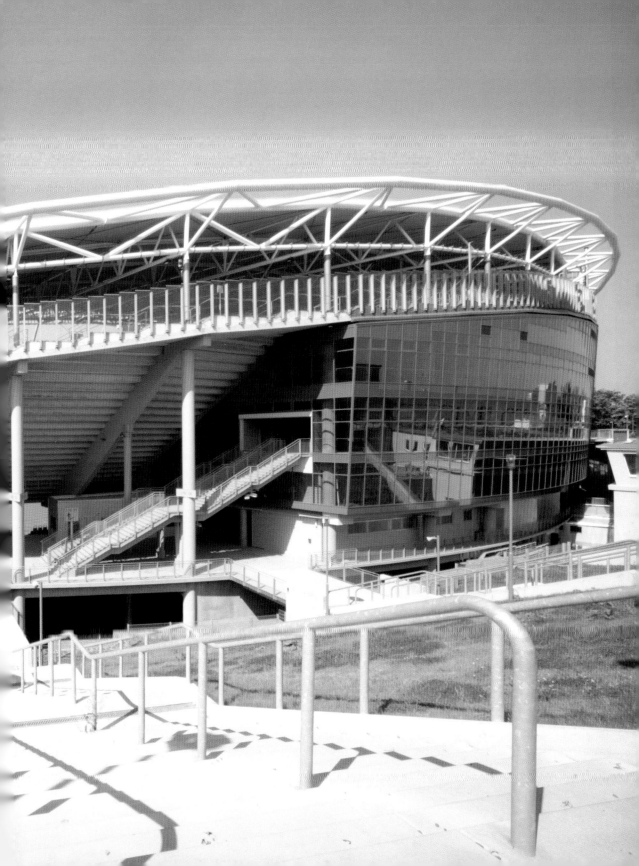

WOOD & ZAPATA, LOHAN CAPRILE GOETTSCH ASSOCIATES | NEW YORK
SOLDIER FIELD STADIUM
www.soldierfield.net
Chicago, Illinois, USA | 2003

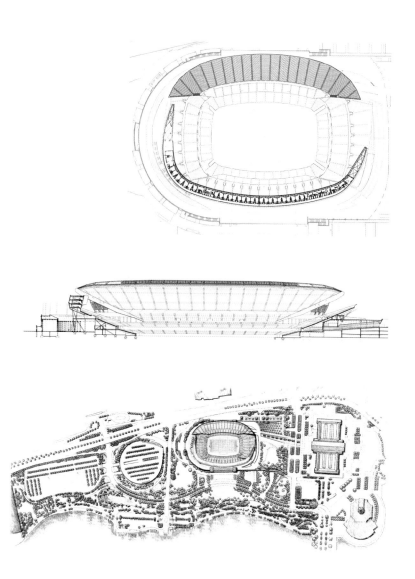

Architekten Arat-Siegel & Partner
Herdweg 64,
70174 Stuttgart, Germany
P +49 711 22 33 80
F +49 711 22 33 888
asp@asp-stuttgart.de
www.asp-stuttgart.de
Gottlieb-Daimler Stadium
© Dirk Wilhelmy

Architekten Schröder Schulte-Ladbeck Strothmann
Heiliger Weg 60,
44135 Dortmund, Germany
P +49 231 91 30 090
F +49 231 91 30 0999
info@planungsgruppe.net
www.planungsgruppe.net
Westfalen Stadium
© Dirk Wilhelmy

Atelier d'Architecture Chaix & Morel et Associés
16 Rue de Haies,
75020 Paris, France
P +33 1 43 70 69 24
F +33 1 43 70 67 65
contact@chaixetmorel.com
www.chaixetmorel.com
Licorne Amiens Stadium
© Christian Richters

Atelier Hitoshi Abe
3-3-16 Oroshimachi, Wakabayashi-ku, Sendai,
984-0015 Miyagi, Japan
P +81 22 284 3411
F +81 22 782 1233
house@a-slash.jp
www.a-slash.jp
Miyagi World Cup Stadium
© MAP system, Shunichi Atsumi

AXS Satow Inc.
AXS Bldg. 2-10-12 Yokoami, Sumida-ku,
130-0015 Tokyo, Japan
P +81 3 5611 7200
F +81 3 56 11 7226
satow@axscom.co.jp
www.axscom.co.jp
Shizuoka Stadium
© Nagoya SS Co., Ltd.

Beyond Space Group
1654-4, Bongcheon-dong, Gwanak-gu,
151-061 Seoul, South Korea
P +82 2 873 2020
F +82 2 873 2025
cau2001@hanmail.net
www.beyondspace.co.kr
Seoul World Cup Main Stadium
© Beyond Space Group

Dominique Perrault
Hôtel Industriel Berlier, 26 rue Bruneseau,
F 75013 Paris, France
P +31 4406 0000
F +31 4406 0001
dominique.perrault@perraultarchitecte.com
www.perraultarchitecte.com
Berlin Olympic Velodrome
© Christian Richters

Eduardo Souto de Moura
Rua de Aleixo 53 1.º A,
4150-043 Porto, Portugal
P +351 22 618 7547
F +351 22 610 8092
souto.moura@mail.telepac.pt
Braga Stadium
© Christian Richters

Hentrich-Petschnigg & Partner KG
Heinrich-Heine-Allee 37,
40213 Düsseldorf, Germany
P +49 211 83 840
F +49 211 83 84 185
info@hpp.com
www.hpp.com
Franken Stadium, Veltins Arena
© Dirk Wilhelmy

Herzog & De Meuron
Rheinschanze 6,
4056 Basel, Switzerland
P +41 61 38 55 758
F +41 61 38 55 757
info@herzogdemeuron.ch
Allianz Arena
© Dirk Wilhelmy

HOK sport & venue & event
300 Wyandotte,
Kansas City, MO 64105, USA
P +1 816 221 1500
F +1 816 221 1578
sport@hok.com
www.hoksve.com
American Ball Park, Gillette Stadium
© Jim Maguire

Idea Image Institute of Architects
4th fl. 5-138 Changjeon-dong, Mapo-ku,
121-880 Seoul, South Korea
P +82 2325 9872
F +82 2325 5692
iiia@chulian.net
www.ideaimage.com
Daegu World Cup Stadium
© Idea Image Institute Of Architects

Kisho Kurokawa Architect & Associates
11th Floor Aoyama Building, 1-2-3 Kita Aoyama, Minato-ku,
107-0061 Tokyo, Japan
P +81 3 3404 3481
F +81 3 3404 6222
kurokawa@kisho.co.jp
www.kisho.co.jp
Oita World Cup Stadium, Toyota City Stadium
© Koji Kobayashi

Manuel Salgado
Travessa do Conde da Ponte 16 A,
1300-141 Lisbon, Portugal
P +351 21 36 104 20
F +351 21 36 10 422
masalgado@risco.org
Dragão Stadium
© Edgar Alves

Mos Architekten
Max-Brauer-Allee 50,
22765 Hamburg, Germany
P +49 40 85 33 46 11
F +49 40 85 33 46 10
AOL Arena
© Dirk Wilhelmy

Nikken Sekkei
2-18-3 Lidabashi, Chiyoda-ku,
102-0072 Tokyo, Japan
P +81 3 5226 3030
F +81 3 5226 3044
webmaster@nikken.co.jp
www.nikken.co.jp
Big Swan Niigata Stadium
© Masuo Kamiyama

NoMad Arquitectos
c/del Pez, 27 1.º izq.,
28004 Madrid, Spain
P +34 91 532 70 34
F +34 91 522 88 47
nomad@nomad.as
www.nomad.as
Lasesarre Football Stadium
© Gogortza & Llorella

Santiago Calatrava
Parkring 11,
8002 Zürich, Switzerland
P +41 44 204 5000
F +41 44 204 5001
www.calatrava.com
Athen Olympic Stadium, Athen Olympic Velodrome
© Burg & Schuh

Schlaich Bergermann & Partner
Hohenzollernstraße 1,
70178 Stuttgart, Germany
P +49 711 64 87 10
F +49 711 64 87 166
info@sbp.de
www.sbp.de
Gottlieb-Daimler Stadium
© Dirk Wilhelmy

Schulitz & Partner Architekten BDA
Viewegstrasse 26,
38102 Braunschweig, Germany
P +49 531 22 07 00
F +49 531 22 07 032
spa@schulitz.de
www.schulitz.de
AWD Arena
© Dirk Wilhelmy

Space Group Architects
219 Wonseo-dong, Jongno-gu,
Seoul, South Korea
P +82 2 763 0771
F +82 2 743 9104
master@spacea.com
www.spacea.com
Busan Asiad Main Stadium
© Myoung Hwan Cho

Tomás Taveira
Av. República 2 1.º andar,
1050-191 Lisbon, Portugal
P +351 21 313 87 70
F +351 21 313 87 94
tomas-taveira-sa@mail.telepac.pt
www.tomas-taveira-proj.pt
Aveiro Stadium, José Alvalade XXI Stadium
© F&S – Guerra

Von Gerkan, Marg & Partner
Elbchaussee 139,
22763 Hamburg, Germany
P +49 40 88 15 10
F +49 40 88 15 1177
hamburg-e@gmp-architekten.de
www.gmp-architekten.de
Berlin Olympia Stadium, Commerzbank Arena,
Rhein Energy Stadium
© Dirk Wilhelmy

Weidleplan Consulting GmbH
Maybachstrasse 33,
70469 Stuttgart, Germany
P +49 711 13 58 0
F +49 711 13 58 300
info@weidleplan.de
www.weidleplan.de
Gottlieb-Daimler Stadium
© Dirk Wilhelmy

Wirth & Wirth Architekten
Funkenburgstrasse 6,
04105 Leipzig, Germany
P +49 341 98 89 90
F +49 341 98 89 919
wirth.leipzig@wirth-wirth.ch
www.wirth-wirth.ch
Zentral Stadium
© Dirk Wilhelmy

Wood & Zapata
444 Broadway,
New York, NY 10013, USA
P +1 212 966 9292
F +1 212 966 9242
mkoff@wood-zapata.com
www.wood-zapata.com
Soldier Field Stadium
© LW&Z Joint Venture

© 2006 daab
cologne london new york

published and distributed worldwide by
daab gmbh
friesenstr. 50
d - 50670 köln

p + 49 - 221 - 94 10 740
f + 49 - 221 - 94 10 741

mail@daab-online.com
www.daab-online.com

publisher ralf daab
rdaab@daab-online.com

creative director feyyaz
mail@feyyaz.com

editorial project by loft publications
© 2006 loft publications

editor and text anja llorella

layout nil solà serra
research martin rolshoven
english translation nadja leonard-mondoloni
french translation marion westerhoff
italian translation sara tonelli
spanish translation almudena sasian
copy editing alessandro orsi

printed in spain
anman gràfiques del vallès, spain
www.anman.com

isbn 3 - 937718 - 38 - 9
d.l. B-2756-06